THEN & NOW®

# THE BRONX

**Opposite:** This photograph shows the High Bridge in 1862, while a large main is being installed to increase the carrying capacity of the Croton Aqueduct System. As a result of cholera epidemics that had ravaged the city since the 18th century, New York City approved an ambitious plan for a new water supply. The Croton Aqueduct System utilized the Croton watershed of upper Westchester County to transport water south. Constructed across the Harlem River, the High Bridge connected the underground aqueducts from Westchester all the way to Manhattan, carrying water to city reservoirs. The bridge's center stone piers were replaced with a single steel span in 1928 to improve navigation on the river. The view looks east into what is today the borough of the Bronx.

# THE BRONX

## Kathleen A. McAuley and Gary Hermalyn

*To Buddy and Isabelle Lee*

Library of Congress Control Number: 2009942703

Published by Arcadia Publishing
Charleston, South Carolina

Printed in the United States of America

Then and Now is a registered trademark and is used under license from
Salamander Books Limited

For all general information contact Arcadia Publishing at:
Telephone 843-853-2070
Fax 843-853-0044
E-mail sales@arcadiapublishing.com
For customer service and orders:
Toll-Free 1-888-313-2665

Visit us on the Internet at www.arcadiapublishing.com

**ON THE FRONT COVER:** Cows graze in a field along East 161st Street in 1904, while New York Central rail cars are parked next to a repair shed opposite it on the south side of the street. It is difficult to imagine that what is today the borough of the Bronx's main corridor of judicial power was once so bucolic. The view looks west; the crest of the hill is along today's Grand Concourse. Today the Mario Merola Bronx County Building stands on the former Gerard Walton Morris estate.

**ON THE BACK COVER:** This late-19th-century photograph shows a substantial-sized private house being prepared for moving. The location is uncertain, although it is known that the firm that undertook the task was Christian Vorndran, professional house movers with an office at 672 East 147th Street in the Bronx. To modern eyes, moving such a house with lumber, manual labor, and teams of horses is quite amazing, although it was done frequently at the time. It was far less expensive to move such a house a short distance than to rebuild it.

# CONTENTS

# ACKNOWLEDGMENTS

The authors wish to acknowledge the following individuals who have contributed to putting together this book: Angel Hernandez of the Bronx County Historical Society, who was instrumental in photographically documenting the Bronx of today; Teresa Brown, Marcus Hickman, Catherine Pellicano, and Laura Tosi of the Bronx County Historical Society; Denise Diaz of the society and Dave Greco of Mike's Deli for providing us with historical and contemporary photographs of Jerome Park and Arthur Avenue, respectively; and Buddy Weiss for his support and advice.

Unless otherwise noted, all images are courtesy of the Bronx County Historical Society.

# INTRODUCTION

This new work is a perfect complement to the changes that involved the Bronx, in particular, and the city of New York and the United States, in general. In fact, oftentimes what happens in the Bronx is reflected in the rest of the country years later. The borough of the Bronx is a microcosm of the nation.

While it is impressive to contrast images of the Macombs Dam Bridge in 1909 against the same site a century later with the new Yankee Stadium dominating the skyline, what perhaps is more remarkable is that photographs taken 100 or more years apart can reveal scenes of the Bronx that are surprisingly bucolic, demonstrating an enduring visage unchanged by modernity. While many of those comparisons are not utilized, it nonetheless demonstrates the relativity of change.

The Bronx was given its name in 1898 when the City of Greater New York was formed. Prior to that, the Bronx was known variously as the Annexed District, the Great North Side, and the 23rd and 24th Wards. When the boroughs of New York City were established (the first time that the borough system was used in the United States), it was decided to name the new borough after its single largest geographical feature: the Bronx River. The Bronx River was named after Jonas Bronck, a Swede from Småland who settled in 1639 near the banks of the river that would one day receive his name. The population of the newly enlarged city of New York was almost 3.5 million, while the population of the Bronx was just over 200,000. Interestingly, by 1925, the borough's population had grown to over 1 million, made up of people from all walks of life. There was even commercial farming still being practiced, especially in the East Bronx. The largest cucumber/pickle works in the country, for example, were based around where Co-op City is today near Eastchester Bay.

The Bronx's recorded history is over 350 years in length; its photographic documentation spans 154 of those years. The earliest known photographic image of the Bronx is of the village of Tremont as it appeared in 1856. These photographs bring a richness and understanding of life in the past that words cannot truly convey, as they join the world of today with our distant past.

# CHAPTER 1

# THE NORTHWEST BRONX

A Bronx victory parade to welcome home the troops from World War I was held along the Grand Concourse on June 14, 1919. The theatrical circuit firm of B. F. Keith was a sponsor, as can be seen on the sign being carried by the young boy walking next to "Uncle Sam." On the left, beyond the people standing along the sidewalk, is the landmark Edgar Allan Poe Cottage, in Poe Park.

The roof of the commercial building at the intersection of Morris Avenue and Fordham Road has served as the locale for huge advertising billboards—seen here currently and in the late 1940s. It is still a lively area of diversified retail businesses, but sadly, five-and-dime variety stores like W. T. Grant Company have gone the way of the horse and buggy.

In 1909, a bronze bust dedicated to Edgar Allan Poe sits in Poe Park, with a fairly empty Grand Concourse behind it. Poe made Fordham his home for the last years of his life (1846–1849). To save the home from destruction, New York City created Poe Park in 1902, bought the house in 1913, and moved it from its original location on the other side of Kingsbridge Road into the north end of the park. The landmark is operated as a historic house museum by the Bronx County Historical Society and is a member of the Historic House Trust of New York City. Today Poe Park is a heavily used green space just over 2 acres in size, with a bandstand at its south end and Poe Cottage at the north. The Poe Park Visitor Center, under construction, is visible between the structures. The center will provide program space for indoor events, interactive exhibitions on Bronx history, and informational kiosks on the Bronx's cultural and commercial offerings.

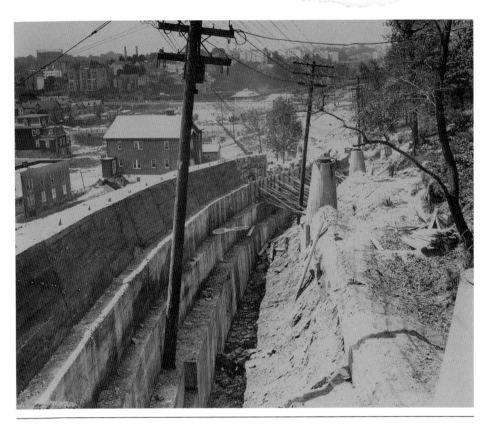

Massive masonry blocks were used during the construction of Riverdale Avenue's retaining wall in 1928. The blocks came from High Bridge's center piers, which had been disassembled to make way for a single steel span to facilitate ship traffic on the Harlem River. Not much has stayed the same in this view, which faces south and east into Marble Hill. The area has been built up with housing and a series of secondary roads serving an ever-enlarging community.

This 1905 photograph looks south along Jerome Avenue, with its pre-elevated line vista, just below the intersection with Mosholu Parkway. The redbrick building on the right is the High Pumping Station. It was constructed as part of the Jerome Park Reservoir complex to pump water from the reservoir located to the west. Opened in 1918, the Jerome Avenue Elevated line, connecting to the Lexington Avenue subway in Manhattan, sparked the development of this Norwood/Mosholu Parkway neighborhood.

This 1907 photograph looks down on Fordham Road as seen from the overhead tracks of the Third Avenue Elevated. At the time of the photograph, the Fordham neighborhood was just coming out of its more rural, peaceful past. Yet the many means of rapid transit available to its inhabitants demonstrated that Fordham was a viable community for those who regularly traveled into Manhattan for work or play, by either the Harlem railroad line, seen below street level, or above it, on the Third Avenue Elevated.

This 1916 photograph shows the home of Civil War brigadier general John Ewen, once located on land overlooking Kingsbridge. Ewen's daughter Eliza donated the property in 1916 to New York City with the understanding that she would remain in her home until her death. Ewen Park, encompassing over 7 acres, links the Kingsbridge and Riverdale neighborhoods by means of a steep stairway opening out onto Riverdale Avenue at West 231st Street. The park's sweeping lawn is a popular spot for sledding in wintertime.

In this early-20th-century photograph, Fordham Road, then a tranquil dirt country road, can be seen looking west from the Grand Concourse. Fordham Road has been a thriving, bustling commercial strip for decades. In the current photograph, the large building on the right is Two Fordham Square, with a conglomeration of business offices, stores, and a branch of the City University of New York. This corner has been home to department stores, such as Caldor's, and more famously, Alexander's Department Store. Between the World Wars, it was the site of the Adams-Wertheimer Department Store.

In 1874, the Valentine-Varian House faces the roadway that was once part of the Colonial-era Boston Post Road and would become Van Cortlandt Avenue East. Posing in front of the house are its occupants: Jesse Huestis Varian; his wife, Lorinda Conklin Varian; and his father, Michael Varian (right). The Valentine-Varian House was built by blacksmith and farmer Isaac Valentine in 1758. The historical landmark saw military action during the Revolutionary War but survived. In 1965, the house was donated to the Bronx County Historical Society and moved diagonally across the street to its present site on a new foundation. It now operates as the Museum of Bronx History. In the current photograph, the apartment building on the left stands on the house's original location. Today it is located across Bainbridge Avenue, set in its own parkland adjacent to Williamsbridge Oval Park.

This block along the east side of the Grand Concourse between East 192nd Street and Fordham Road was photographed in 1932, the same year its appearance changed dramatically. The apartment building near the end of the street was demolished for the main building of Dollar Savings Bank at 2530 Grand Concourse, followed in 1951 by the tower structure attached to it. Over the years, the entire street has been transformed; only the apartment building near its north end and the attached row of shops at the corner with Fordham Road remain.

In 1905, excavation is underway for the Jerome Park Reservoir. The reservoir takes its name from the 19th-century racetrack that once stood there. In 1866, Leonard Jerome, a wealthy financier and future grandfather of Winston Churchill, helped organize the American Jockey Club and the racetrack. For almost 30 years, the area was dominated by the racecourse. In its heyday, Jerome Park was a magnet for the rich, famous, and fashionable. The early photograph shows a view north to the parade ground of Van Cortlandt Park and west toward Riverdale and beyond, to the Palisades of New Jersey. The modern photograph is taken from Scott Tower on Paul Avenue. (Now photograph courtesy of Denise Diaz.)

Broadway at West 242nd Street is full of busy trolley, automobile, and foot traffic in 1921. The view from the terminus station of the Broadway Elevated line looks north, with Van Cortlandt Park on the right. The subway route was built in sections; the final piece, from 230th Street to 242nd Street, opened in 1908. To encourage settlement, realty firms emphasized easy access to mass transit. This location was once the heart of Mosholu village, known in the 1850s as Warnerville, with a general store, blacksmith and wagon shops, a schoolhouse, a Methodist church, and a cluster of homes.

A 1928 view looks west and north along the Harlem River Ship Canal toward the proposed site of the Henry Hudson Bridge. Officially opened in 1895, the canal, known also as the United States Ship Canal, helped connect the Hudson and Harlem Rivers for maritime traffic. The building of the canal reshaped the geography of the area by cutting through the northern tip of Manhattan Island. The section would become known as Marble Hill and joined to the Bronx.

This mid-1940s photograph taken from the Henry Hudson Bridge shows Spuyten Duyvil. Robert Moses, New York City parks commissioner and the ex-officio sole member of the Henry Hudson Parkway Authority, was responsible for the construction of the parkway and bridge. The bridge, parkway, and Henry Hudson Park all commemorate the 1609 visit of the English explorer on the *Half Moon* to a point close to the present-day bridge. On the crest of the hill can be seen the Hudson monument. The 100-foot Doric column and base were constructed in 1912. A monumental bronze sculpture by Karl Bitter was added to the column in 1938.

In case anyone was unable to read the large sign painted onto its roof, the Wager Hotel had plenty of other advertisements to encourage people to stay overnight or just eat and drink in their restaurant. This 1902 photograph shows this large house during a part of its long existence when it was a public hostelry. It still remains across the street from Woodlawn Cemetery on East 233rd Street near Napier Avenue, but today it is a private residence.

The Howard-Valentine house with the portico, on the west side of Marion Avenue just north of Fordham Road, is seen here in 1934, the same year the 19th-century house was sold to real estate developers and then demolished for construction of the apartment building seen in the center of the current image. It was dwarfed by apartment buildings and on the left by what was then the Bainbridge Avenue branch of the New York Public Library. The library ran through the block from Bainbridge Avenue. It served as the borough's main branch until a new gleaming steel and glass facility opened in 2006 at 310 East Kingsbridge Road. The Howards were related by marriage to the Valentine family, who owned a farm along what is today Valentine Avenue north of East 194th Street.

Trolley service ran right up to the northern boundary of New York City. Pictured here in the early 1920s is the intersection of Webster and McLean Avenues, the boundary with Yonkers in Westchester County. The Union Railway trolley, seen on the left, went south through the Bronx and eventually across the Willis Avenue Bridge into Manhattan. To the right of the intersection is the Nereid Avenue overpass above the Harlem line railroad tracks. The overpass leads into the Northeast Bronx and the community of Wakefield.

King's Bridge was still in use when this photograph was taken in 1913, looking north and west up to the heights of Riverdale. Built in 1693, it spanned Spuyten Duyvil Creek, which separated upper Manhattan from what is today the Bronx. During the Revolutionary War, it was the main military artery for both sides and was under continuous attack. The bridge survived until 1916, when Spuyten Duyvil Creek was filled in. Today the site is south of the intersection of West 230th Street and Kingsbridge Avenue.

The Bolton home at 351 Bedford Park Boulevard at Marion Avenue is seen here about 1920. For generations, the Bolton family lived at the site of what is today the Bronx Zoo. The Bolton Bleaching and Manufacturing Company was established in 1822 along the Bronx River, together with what became the village of Bronxdale for its workers. Water from the Bronx River was used in various processes and, supplemented by steam, supplied the power. In the late 1880s, the Bronxdale property was condemned for the creation of Bronx Park and with it, the Bronx Zoo.

A woman poses in 1915 under the steel framework of Kingsbridge Armory's 180,000-square-foot drill floor. Taking five years to build (1912–1917), the armory was home for decades to the New York State National Guard's 258th Field Artillery unit. The armory played host to boat shows, musical concerts, rodeos, bicycle races, track meets, and trade and other commercial exhibitions. The massive nine-story redbrick building encompasses an entire block running along Jerome Avenue from Kingsbridge Road to East 195th Street and west to Reservoir Avenue. With nationwide military cutbacks in the 1990s, the armory's ownership was transferred over by the state to New York City in 1996. Now a historical landmark, plans for its future use have included educational space and development into a shopping mall.

This 1932 bird's-eye view shows Mosholu Parkway at the northern end of the Grand Concourse. The parkway is an important landscaped roadway linking Van Cortlandt and Bronx Parks. The name *Mosholu*, meaning "small stones" or "smooth stones," was the Algonquin name for what is known today as Tibbett's Brook.

Soldiers of the U.S. Army Medical Department, Ambulance, and Stretcher Bearer Corps stand at attention in 1918 along Bainbridge Avenue just south of Montefiore Hospital. Athletic fields owned by Columbia University just north of the hospital were taken over by the military during World War I to build a training hospital known as "Camp Seuss" or, officially, as Chateau Thierry, after the French World War I battlefield. Today the neighborhood is dominated by the hospital complex of Montefiore Medical Center, Moses Division.

# CHAPTER 2

# THE NORTHEAST BRONX

Eden Terrace is seen about 1907, with a view west from Boston Road over Rattlesnake Creek. This formed the lower boundary of John H. Eden's estate, called "Edenwald," the name being noted on 1903 and 1910 maps. Rattlesnake Creek, also known as Rattlesnake Brook, flowed alongside this street until the 1960s. Eden Terrace was changed to Marolla Terrace in 1968 to honor a local resident prominent in Little League baseball activities.

Kilian Breinlinger purchased this 4-acre picnic and recreational resort, seen here in the 1940s, along Boston Road where Dyre Avenue would eventually be cut through. It had been known as Dickert's Old Point Comfort Park and could accommodate 2,000–3,000 visitors at a time for weddings, banquets, and the annual Oktoberfest celebrations. The wooden main building was torn down in 1960; the park itself operated through 1957. It is believed that the structure was on the site of a Revolutionary War–era inn.

When this photograph, looking west, was taken in 1924, there was very little to see at this location other than the White Plains Road Elevated line and its Allerton Avenue station. The photograph was used to enhance a real estate prospectus for the sale of the Hammersley Estate that ran from Boston Road to Allerton Avenue. The property belonged to the Honeywell family in the 18th century.

The Russell family maintained a large farm stand and plant nursery in the 1940s and into the 1950s at the intersection of Eastchester and Gun Hill Roads. The East Bronx maintained a more rural feel and contained scattered farm plots until after World War II. This location is also referred to as "Givan's Square," in honor of Robert Givan, an early-19th-century miller whose estate was just to the east.

In March 1953, this bare, undeveloped patch of ground marks the future Tiemann Avenue, looking north from Mace Avenue toward Gun Hill Road. It is in the process of being cut through to bring it into line with the street system. The avenue is named for Daniel Fawcett Tiemann, a wealthy paint manufacturer, who served as New York City's mayor from 1858 to 1860.

This photograph shows workers during the late 1920s at the Nevins Shipyard on City Island. Henry B. Nevins (1878–1959) was a master yacht builder. In 1907, he bought Adam Hansen's boatyard on land that had once been the City Island Athletic Club. The structures fronted on the east side of City Island Avenue, between Winters and Centre Streets. The Nevins Shipyard was renowned for the construction of custom-made cruising and racing yachts and other small craft and minesweepers for the war effort during World War II. Today the site of the shipyard is taken up by P.S. 175 (the City Island School) and the playground next to it.

The famous 19th-century coloratura soprano Adelina Patti spent part of her youth in what is now considered Wakefield. She lived on Matilda Avenue in a house that still exists north of East 241st Street and is depicted in this late-19th-century image. Named for the birthplace of George Washington, Wakefield was surveyed in 1853; its boundaries were from present-day East 215th Street to East 233rd Street, from the Bronx River to just about Laconia Avenue. When New York City annexed Wakefield in 1895, the community's boundaries were stretched north to East 243rd Street to include the hamlets of Jacksonville and Washingtonville.

This 19th-century photograph of the Vincent-Halsey House shows off the property's ornate stone gateway. Its main claim to fame is that it was occupied by Abigail Adams and Col. William Smith. Pres. John Adams, Abigail's father, stayed at the house for two months in 1797 to escape a yellow fever epidemic in Philadelphia. Having been moved three times in its long history, it was originally located near the present-day intersection of Boston Road and Conner Street.

This rural scene from the 1890s shows Bussing Avenue looking east from Baychester Avenue. The rustic bridge in the middle distance crosses Rattlesnake Creek. The waterway flowed through Seton Falls Park under Boston Road and emptied into Long Pond off the Hutchinson River. It was finally covered over for Freedomland Amusement Park. Bussing Avenue was part of the original Boston Post Road and before that was a Native American pathway that led south to Gun Hill Road.

This late-19th-century photograph of City Island shows the horse-drawn trolley car traveling north along City Island Avenue, the main thoroughfare. The car is standing at the northwest corner of the avenue at Fordham Street. With one set of tracks, the trolley car went up and down City Island one trip at a time. Today the island is still quite low-key and has the feel of a small town if one ignores the automobiles. City Island is often compared in lifestyle and local color to a New England fishing village.

The William Thwaite's Hotel and Old Homestead Tavern was a 19th-century fixture in Bronxdale Village. According to an 1897 atlas, the house fronted part of the old White Plains Road at approximately Barker Avenue between Thwaites Place and Reiss Place, just north of today's Pelham Parkway. Today White Plains Road, incorporating some parts of the original roadway, is located to the east and is dominated by the presence of the White Plains Road Elevated line.

An aerial photograph of the Freedomland Amusement Park site shows the property contoured into the shape of the continental United States. Although the amusement park lasted a brief time—ground-breaking took place in 1959, it declared bankruptcy in September 1964, and was torn down in early 1965—Freedomland holds some very fond memories for many New York–area baby boomers. The location of the park is now occupied by Co-op City and the Bay Plaza Shopping Center.

This 1903 view shows a rural East 233rd Street as it rises from Webster Avenue up into Wakefield. In the foreground is the New York Central's Harlem Har, its tracks still dangerously at ground level. Today the intersection is much busier, with 233rd Street a main east-west conduit for Bronx River Parkway and Major Deegan Expressway traffic. Up the hill, on the right, is the former Our Lady of Mercy Medical Center, now referred to as Montefiore Medical Center, North Division.

The construction of the Edenwald housing complex had only just begun when this photograph was taken in May 1951. The wooded view looks north toward Grenada Place. In the foreground, the foundation for 1145 East 229th Street is taking shape. Edenwald Houses, completed in October 1953, is the largest New York City Housing Authority development in the Bronx, with 40 buildings.

Worried about child safety, mothers protest the lack of adequate traffic lights around the perimeters of the Pelham Parkway Houses sometime in the 1950s. The 23.74-acre housing complex was completed in June 1950. Consisting of 23 six-story buildings, the project is bordered by Pelham Parkway, Williamsbridge Road, and Mace and Wallace Avenues. A century ago, this land was part of the William Waldorf Astor and Lorillard Spencer estates. The broad, tree-lined Pelham Parkway to its south has helped shape the community.

This early-20th-century photograph shows Willett Avenue in Williamsbridge, looking south from about East 216th Street. The Willetts were property owners in the area during the 19th century and no doubt were the source of the street name. Although some newer housing has come into the street, it is generally in keeping with the small-scale feel of the neighborhood. Many single-family houses still remain from a century ago. Unfortunately the canopy of trees no longer exists.

This 1914 photograph shows Boston Road, looking south, with the tracks of the New York, Westchester, and Boston Railroad overhead. The wooden barn, with its alarm bell on the roof, was home to the Defender Hose Company No. 1. This volunteer fire company helped serve the community in Eastchester until it was disbanded in 1923. The rail tracks were later taken over for use by New York City's Dyre Avenue Elevated line.

This photograph shows adults and children in the late 1940s or early 1950s waiting to see Santa Claus during a Christmas tribute presented by the Gun Hill-Eastchester Board of Trade. They stand on an empty lot on the east side of Gun Hill Road at Fenton Avenue and Knapp Street. A row of stores and the Gun Hill Road station of the Dyre Avenue subway line are across the street. Today the lot is occupied by the Eastchester branch of the New York Public Library.

Peter Riess and his wife pose in the 1890s in front of their house along the west side of the original Newell Street in Olinville. The Riess property was part of land that was long ago obliterated by the construction of the Bronx River Parkway's southbound lanes. Peter had maintained a fur-dyeing business since 1882 in the small building behind his house.

The construction of Co-op City is well underway in August 1968, as seen from the beach along the Hutchinson River. What is today referred to as Baychester was once part of the old settlement of Eastchester. The area became home for a short time to Freedomland Amusement Park, a $65-million recreational concept built on acres of reclaimed swampland and creeks that were part of the original Pell Grant of the 17th century. Construction of Co-op City began in 1968 and was completed in 1971. With over 15,000 apartments spread through 42 high-rise buildings and townhouses, Co-op City became about the largest single residential development in the United States.

CHAPTER 3

# THE SOUTHEAST
# BRONX

Just off Bruckner Boulevard, around Soundview Avenue on Clason Point, was a whole community of Quonset huts, seen here in 1946. These were erected on open land as a temporary measure by the New York City Housing Authority to accommodate returning World War II veterans and their growing families. Each hut could house two separate families that domesticated their surroundings as best they could. Conditions, however, were rather cramped.

A schooner unloads its cargo in the early 20th century at the dock along Westchester Creek just south of today's East Tremont Avenue. These ships navigated up Westchester Creek from the East River. Beyond the dock is the office and yard of Sidney Bowne and Son, dealing in coal, lumber, and other building materials. Today the area is mostly covered over with the athletic field of Herbert H. Lehman High School. For a waterway that was so instrumental in the development and prosperity of Westchester Township, it is difficult to even discern Westchester Creek, obscured by the Hutchinson River Parkway.

In May 1939, when this photograph was taken, the Hollow Tavern sits alone and rather forlorn below the grade of Unionport Road just south of East Tremont Avenue. This is one of a series of photographs taken for the Metropolitan Life Insurance Company to document the site development and construction of Parkchester. The buildings are about to rise across the street and behind the tavern. There is construction already well underway in other parts of the development. The Hollow Tavern, soon to be dwarfed by its new neighbor, looks like a relic of the past.

This photograph was taken on April 1, 1918, along Eastern (now Bruckner) Boulevard south of Jarvis Street during sewer construction. Although the Jarvis name goes back locally to the 1840s, the street is probably named for Henry J. Jarvis, president of the Chester Taxpayers' Alliance, which lobbied for the rapid transit system extension north into their community. Until the work was completed in 1920, a trip by public transportation to Manhattan from the area required a minimum two-fare, 10¢ fee.

A girls' rope-skipping contest is held in 1923 on the front lawn of the former Adee Mansion in Edgewater Park. The house is now used by the Edgewater Park Volunteer Hose Company No. 1. George Townsend Adee purchased the 35-acre country estate; the stone mansion was built in 1856 with an addition in 1860. The property was later rented to Richard Shaw, an Irish immigrant who rented out land to campers. Edgewater Park, which began as a summer bungalow colony before the 1920s, grew into a permanent settlement.

In 1952, there was little to see along Morris Park Avenue, as it led east and downhill to the intersection with Eastchester Road. The area today is crowded with professional offices, high-rise housing, the major medical institutions of Jacobi Medical Center (to the left, out of camera view), the Albert Einstein College of Medicine, and the Jack Weiler Division of Montefiore Medical Center (right). In the distance is part of the Hutchinson Metro Center, a modern complex of commercial office space, medical and diagnostic facilities, and a branch of Mercy College.

This photograph of the Bronx Gas and Electric Company building at Westchester Square and Frisby Avenue may date from May 1916. With the bunting and large sign reading, "The Best Is None Too Good—The East Bronx," these people may be celebrating the May 27, 1916, ground-breaking for the last section of the Pelham Bay Elevated line. It was built in stages up to Pelham Bay Park Station and opened on December 20, 1920. The line served as a catalyst for residential development in the East Bronx. The school building of P.S. 12 can be seen up Frisby Avenue; today its more modern building fronts on Tratman Avenue.

These aerial views show the New York Catholic Protectory in 1937 and Parkchester, which now occupies the site. The protectory was an institution established after the Civil War for orphaned and abandoned children. The 150-acre property was bisected by Unionport Road, which also served as a dividing line between facilities for its boys and girls. They were taught useful skills such as letterpress printing, carpentry, blacksmithing, embroidery and sewing, cooking, and agriculture. The Metropolitan Life Insurance Company bought the property in 1938 to build Parkchester, a self-contained middle-class planned community.

East Tremont Avenue is seen in 1909 as it intersects with Commonwealth Avenue alongside the tracks of the New York, New Haven, and Hartford Railroad to the left. In the 19th century, Tremont Avenue had different names as it made its way across what is today the Bronx.

This stretch of the road, from the Bronx River to Castle Hill Avenue, was named Walker Avenue after a wealthy Quaker family by the same name. Remarkably, this stretch of houses has basically remained the same for over 100 years, modern aluminum siding notwithstanding.

This 1906 photograph shows White Plains Road as it meets the East River on Clason Point. At the turn of the 20th century, the Higgs family maintained a beach camp there, while an adjoining picnic area and pavilion was called Killian's Grove. In the 1920s, both were incorporated into the bungalow colony that was named in honor of Pres. Warren G. Harding. After World War II, these became permanent year-round residences.

In 1918, New York City mayor John F. Hylan is welcomed with a big sign at Phil Dietrich's restaurant and tavern at Gildersleeve and Soundview Avenues, near the foot of Clason Point. Nearby was Kane's, a popular resort of the early 1900s that was famous for its political outings, clambakes, civic rallies, gymnastic exhibitions, dance marathons, and brass band concerts.

This 1930s photograph shows a wide swath of undeveloped land along the east bank of the Bronx River in Soundview. The street in the distance is Watson Avenue looking east as seen in the current photograph from Bronx River Avenue. Watson Avenue recalls William Watson, a local mid-19th-century landowner whose estate encompassed this area. His beautiful stone mansion was located near Elder and Westchester Avenues.

THE SOUTHEAST BRONX

Gilbert Merritt stands on a "disappearing gun" in 1927 at Fort Schuyler on Throgs Neck. These heavy artillery pieces were designed to retract into bunkers to protect them against enemy fire. Fort Schuyler never had to use its weaponry in combat however. The fort, constructed between 1833 and 1845, was intended to close the western end of the Long Island Sound and help protect New York from sea attacks. After 1870, the fort saw only marginal use before closing in 1911. It was leased in 1931 for the New York State Merchant Marine Academy. Restoration began under the Works Progress Administration in 1934–1938; the fort was gutted to accommodate dormitories, offices, and classrooms. Today it is home to the State University of New York Maritime College.

This photograph, taken in 1920, shows East Tremont Avenue, looking west in Schuylerville. The trolley has just passed the intersection of Eastern Boulevard. In 1942, the road's name was changed to Bruckner Boulevard in honor of Henry Bruckner, Bronx borough president from 1918 to 1933. Along this busy strip, there is little that remains from the 1920s, but a close look reveals the small house with the mansard roof still standing on the right.

This early-20th-century photograph looks toward the corner of Van Nest and Wallace Avenues. The community of Van Nest took its name from the local depot of the New York, New Haven, and Hartford Railroad. Reynier Van Nest's son Abraham was a director of the line who wanted to honor the memory of his father. The station began service for those enjoying the Morris Park racetrack.

This 1920s photograph shows Schneider-Sampson Memorial Square, today known as Schneider-Sampson Park, bounded by Bruckner Boulevard and Baisley and Hollywood Avenues. The triangle honors two Schuylerville residents who were victims of World War I, and it became parkland in 1929. George Schneider, a star of the Franklin Athletic Club on Blondell Avenue, was killed in action in 1918. William P. Sampson, a machine gunner, was gassed in August 1918 but survived the war. He died some 11 years later of pneumonia at the age of 33.

This view, part of a 1929–1930 panoramic photograph, shows people lining up at Spooner's Beach facing the Long Island Sound to watch the dynamiting of an offshore wreck. The sign announces it as the future site of the Bronx Beach Club. This stretch of beach next to Locust Point was formed when John T. Wright extended a causeway out to Wright's Island (now Locust Point) that was the property of his father, Capt. George Wright. Today the approximate location is the site of the Throgs Neck Bridge's tollbooths.

This 1939 view looks up Unionport Road where it intersects with Olmstead Avenue just north of Westchester Avenue. In the distance, Parkchester is under construction. On the left is the Koterba Vehicle Company, believed to have been the site in the mid–19th century of the Centerville African Methodist Episcopal Church and its adjoining cemetery. By the beginning of the 20th century, the church and cemetery seen on early maps ceased to be noted at that location.

Woodmansten Inn, seen here about 1920, opened in 1906 and was a famous roadhouse in Morris Park during the first quarter of the 20th century. Well-known dance orchestras and entertainers were featured until it was destroyed by fire in 1930. Although the property once extended up to Morris Park Avenue, most of the structure itself straddled the roadbed of Van Nest Avenue, between Tomlinson Avenue and Williamsbridge Road.

A ceremony to dedicate a memorial to Revolutionary War soldiers whose remains were found at Fort Independence was held on June 12, 1927, at St. Peter's Episcopal Church. St. Peter's, one of the oldest parishes in New York, was founded in 1693 and once included the settlements of Westchester, Yonkers, Pelham Manor, and Eastchester. The present St. Peter's Church is the third on the site; the first burnt down in 1788 and was replaced in 1795. That structure was replaced in 1855 by the Gothic-style church designed by Leopold Eidlitz. After a fire destroyed parts of it, the church was rededicated in 1879.

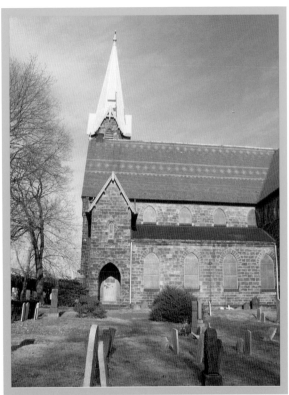

This 1946 aerial view shows the intersection at Soundview, Underhill, and Patterson Avenues on Clason Point. In the center is the Woodrow Wilson Square, later renamed the Woodrow Wilson Triangle. New York City acquired the property in 1912, and it became part of the city's park system in 1927. A monument honors the Clason Point residents who died in World War I. The 7-foot-high bronze sculptural relief by James Novelli is set within a granite stele.

This 1913 photograph shows Morris Park Racetrack; the clubhouse would have been located along the east side of Fowler Avenue, between Morris Park and Van Nest Avenues seen here. The famous racetrack was built to replace Jerome Park Racetrack, which was closed to make way for the Jerome Park Reservoir. By 1902, the Morris Park Racetrack closed for horse racing and was used for a few years for automobile racing until it was sold to real estate developers. Financial problems prompted New York City to take it over in 1907. The city then leased it for two years to the Aeronautic Society of New York, which hosted the first public air show on the grounds. The selling off of the racecourse property in 1913 helped develop the Morris Park community.

# THE SOUTHWEST BRONX

This late-19th-century view of Morrisania shows a row of breweries, including Eichler Brewery, on the crest of the hill at Third Avenue and East 169th Street. German immigrant John Eichler came to New York in 1853 and became involved in the brewery business. He went on to own the Kolb Brewery, and from that he established the Eichler Brewery. By 1888, Eichler's was considered the best equipped in America. The street in the foreground is Washington Avenue, north of East 169th Street. The building on the far left, once a Presbyterian church, housed Tilburn's Pickle Factory.

75

This 1892 photograph shows workers outside the Jordan L. Mott Iron Works building. The community of Mott Haven first appeared in 1828 when Jordan L. Mott, inventor of a cooking stove that was fueled by anthracite coal, opened a factory at Third Avenue and what is today East 134th Street along the Harlem River. The foundry expanded several times over the years to produce a variety of mundane iron goods and ornamental ironwork and fountains that survive today. The company's name is in brick relief on the south facade of the Mott building, which stands next to the Third Avenue Bridge.

This 1890s photograph shows East 149th Street at Morris Avenue with a view to the west. As shown, 149th Street is being regraded—the cone structures are sewer openings. Today the intersection is dominated by Lincoln Medical and Mental Health Center, better known as Lincoln Hospital. With its long tradition of caring for the poor and disadvantaged in New York City, Lincoln Hospital is known for innovative programs addressing community health issues and has the busiest single-site emergency room in the region.

Taken in December 1903, this view looks north along Cedar Avenue to the imposing Webb Academy and Home for Shipbuilders, erected by naval architect and shipbuilder William H. Webb. A local landmark for over 60 years, it served as a training center for young men learning the art of shipbuilding as well as a home for retired seamen and their spouses. The spire just beyond it is part of the Roman Catholic Orphan Asylum, a 30-acre complex opened in 1902. Today Fordham Heights is very different, although a part of it is still used for institutional purposes. The Webb Academy was replaced by the Fordham Hill Houses apartment complex in 1949. The James J. Peters Veterans Affairs Medical Center now occupies the site of the orphan asylum.

THE SOUTHWEST BRONX

This 1906 photograph shows a multiyear construction project to create a sewer system from Claremont Park west to the Harlem River. The view is from Webster Avenue, looking east along Wendover Avenue (today Claremont Parkway) where the buggy is traveling. The structure to the right was then known as the Claremont Hotel. Today much has changed, although the streets remain wide and majestic as they sweep down from the park. The hotel building still stands minus its cupola.

THE SOUTHWEST BRONX

In June 1957, sisters Kathleen (left) and Mary McAuley pose in the Children's Zoo section of the Bronx Zoo. Today a more modernized Children's Zoo offers a wide variety of interactive experiences such as animal feeding, life with prairie dogs, and riding on the Bug Carousel. In the 18th and 19th centuries, as many as a dozen mills producing paper, flour, cloth, pottery, tapestries, barrels, and snuff harnessed the natural hydraulic power of the Bronx River.

This 1856 panoramic view is believed to be the oldest known photograph of what is today the Bronx. The camera was set up on Mount Hope Hill (today the Grand Concourse); the view looks east down into the village of Tremont. Tremont Avenue is the roadway along the white picket fence. Running across the photograph just below the center is the Mill Brook. Today the brook flows under Webster Avenue. It is believed that the generally accepted origin of the name Tremont for this area was chosen by the town's first postmaster, Hiram Tarbox, because three hills were in the town's vicinity: Mount Hope, Mount Eden, and Fairmount.

This *c.* 1901 photograph shows the Peabody Home for Aged Women on Boston Road at Glover Street (today East 179th Street) in West Farms. That location has played a colorful part in Bronx history. The old building on the right, the original part of the home, began in the 1840s as the Mapes Temperance House Hotel. During the Revolutionary War, the site was believed to be the location of Colonel DeLancey's blockhouse, destroyed by American forces led by Col. Aaron Burr. DeLancey, an American who remained loyal to the British, lived along the Bronx River, now in the southern end of the Bronx Zoo. Today the newer portion of the structure remains and is operated as a venue for a variety of community and social assistance programs.

Step streets have been a way of life for Bronxites, especially in the West Bronx with its steep hills. This 1907 photograph looks west down the steps leading toward Cedar Avenue. The Morris Heights stations for the New York Central and the New York and Putnam Railroads are to the left of the intersection down by the Harlem River, where the tracks of both lines once ran parallel to each other. Now only the Metro-North tracks remain; the station can be seen through the trees on the right. The Major Deegan Expressway lies below grade in front of the station's platform.

This 1916 photograph was taken from the west side of Park Avenue at East 189th Street looking east. The Harlem Railroad line is below grade level in the center of the image. Beyond is the Third Avenue Elevated. Some of Fordham University's buildings can be seen in the distance. The Third Avenue Elevated (the "El") was the first rapid transit line in the Bronx. Opened in 1886, the El sparked the development of the central core of the South Bronx. For decades, the Third Avenue El provided basic mobility for millions of Bronxites. In 1955, it was closed in Manhattan and as far up as 149th Street, and all service in the Bronx ended in 1973.

THE SOUTHWEST BRONX

Workers are seen cutting through Park Street (Cauldwell Avenue) north toward Westchester Avenue in 1914. Beyond the elevated line on the right is the original Lebanon Hospital. The structure was built in the 1850s as the Ursuline Convent and Academy for Girls and remained so until 1888, when the Ursuline Sisters moved north to Bedford Park. The building was incorporated in 1892 as Lebanon Hospital and opened the following year for the care of all races and creeds. The old Lebanon Hospital was closed in 1943 after construction of its new facility on the Grand Concourse and Mount Eden Parkway. In 1956, it was torn down and its site prepared for the construction of the St. Mary's Park Houses complex seen here.

This mid-1950s photograph of the Fairmount TV and Appliance Company at the corner of Bathgate and East Tremont Avenues recalls a time when televisions were only just becoming popular in American homes. The small box-like models that were then available are displayed in the window. The wonderful old building that housed the store is gone, replaced by a row of medical offices. In the distance, a small part of Crotona Park can be glimpsed.

Southern Boulevard at Westchester Avenue is seen in 1921 with the elevated tracks of the White Plains Road and Dyre Avenue lines on the left. The apartment building on the right is part of the ARECO development. The American Real Estate Company was a real estate developer that built an impressive range of housing stock in this and adjoining areas in the first decades of the 20th century. Its advertisements emphasized locations convenient to rapid transit into Manhattan, the quality workmanship that went into their construction, and the wide array of modern conveniences available.

This 1932 view, looking north and east, shows the intersection of Davidson Avenue and West 183rd Street. The 183rd Street station of the Jerome Avenue line is down the street. The street name recalls Mathias Davidson, a local landowner in the 1870s. The variety of retail shops on this University Heights street has not changed much, although the prices have, as can be seen on the advertising signs at the corner grocery store.

In 1908, this was the Hunts Point station designed by Cass Gilbert for the New York, New Haven, and Hartford Railroad line. Hunts Point got its name from one of its original 17th-century settlers, Thomas Hunt, who acquired the land through treaties with the Native Americans. Although Hunts Point was a separate village until the 1874 annexation of the West Bronx by New York City, the area throughout most of the 19th and early 20th centuries was known for its large farming estates and imposing mansions of prominent New Yorkers. Local streets such as Casanova, Barretto, Spofford, Faile, Hunt, and others recall these estate owners who once lived in the area.

This 1909 photograph, taken from the newly completed Grand Concourse, looks west and north down East 161st Street toward the Macombs Dam Bridge. The magnificent design of the Grand Concourse was the creation of visionary engineer Louis Risse. He was the chief engineer of the Topographical Bureau in the Office of Commissioner of Street Improvements of the Annexed District in the 23rd and 24th Wards. Today the Grand Boulevard and Concourse (its full, official name) is closely lined with governmental buildings and a few private houses, but mostly apartment buildings, many of them created in the heyday of the art deco movement of the 1930s. This modern view encompasses both old and new Yankee Stadiums.

This 1890 photograph shows East 150th Street and Third Avenue. The young boy is crossing the street toward Rae's Hotel, a stagecoach stop dating back to the 1850s that had a beer garden called Melrose Park behind it. West of the Third Avenue Elevated line is the Roman Catholic Church of the Immaculate Conception of the Blessed Virgin Mary, its brick structure dating from the 1880s. The church and school complex have survived for over a century, although the church's elegant steeple, a longtime neighborhood landmark, was removed in the late 1990s due to deterioration.

This view looks north on Arthur Avenue from the intersection of Crescent Avenue about 1932. Before the establishment of the Arthur Avenue Retail Market building, spearheaded by New York City mayor Fiorello LaGuardia, fresh fruits, vegetables, and dry goods were sold in an open-air market along Arthur Avenue. Maria Cappiello, the photograph donor's grandmother, is in the center of the image in a white dress. Across the street at 2320 Arthur Avenue is the family's store, Cappiello Brothers Butcher. Known also as "Little Italy of the Bronx," Arthur Avenue remains the vibrant historical and commercial center of Belmont, the place to go to for specialty meats, cheeses, gifts, and fine Italian restaurants. The name Belmont comes from the 19th-century Jacob Lorillard estate of the same name that encompassed most of the current community. Arthur Avenue may have been named after either Pres. Chester A. Arthur or Arthur Hoffman, a local city surveyor in the 19th century. (Courtesy of David Greco, Mike's Deli, and Butchie.)

In 1908, the granite Beaux-Arts Bronx Borough Courthouse had begun to rise on this triangular plot of land bounded by East 161st Street and Brook and Third Avenues. The Third Avenue El tracks are beyond. G. E. Roine's monumental sculpture *Justice* graces the courthouse's south facade. Construction began during the Haffen administration, yet it didn't formally open until 1914, with some interior work still needing to be completed. Unused as a courthouse since the 1970s, it remains a Bronx architectural gem.

Mc. Comb's Park, Ball Ground, N. Y. City.

This 1922 postcard shows a baseball game in Macombs Dam Park's ball field. The park was named for the 19th-century Macomb family who operated a dam and mill on the site. The park opened in 1899, drawing neighborhood children and aspiring athletes to its extensive recreational facilities. The construction of a new Yankee Stadium absorbed the park. The ballpark's ground-breaking ceremonies took place on August 16, 2006. During construction, the Yankees continued to play in the original stadium. Although a modern ballpark, the design for the new Yankee Stadium pays tribute to its past, with many interior and exterior design elements inspired by the "House That Ruth Built."

In 1902, workmen lay down trolley tracks into the cobblestone street at East 138th Street where Lincoln, Morris, and Third Avenues converge in Mott Haven. With increased modernization of roadbeds, trolley car lines that ran throughout the Bronx and into Manhattan helped transport Bronxites in an ever-widening circle. The photograph shows the west side of the street north of the intersection. Today only the two northernmost buildings survive from that earlier time.

# Discover Thousands of Local History Books Featuring Millions of Vintage Images

Arcadia Publishing, the leading local history publisher in the United States, is committed to making history accessible and meaningful through publishing books that celebrate and preserve the heritage of America's people and places.

## Find more books like this at
## www.arcadiapublishing.com

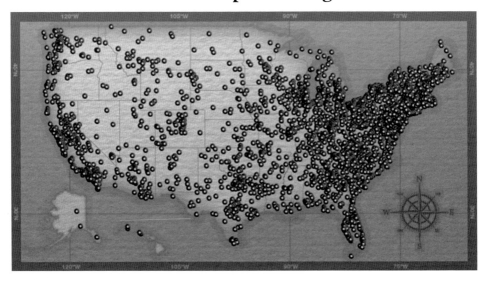

Search for your hometown history, your old stomping grounds, and even your favorite sports team.